Original title:
The Strength to Stay

Copyright © 2024 Swan Charm
All rights reserved.

Author: Swan Charm
ISBN HARDBACK: 978-9916-89-820-8
ISBN PAPERBACK: 978-9916-89-821-5
ISBN EBOOK: 978-9916-89-822-2

Graceful Endurance

In shadows deep, we walk in light,
His guiding hand, our hearts ignite.
Through trials faced, we stand as one,
With strength bestowed, our race begun.

Each tear a prayer, each burden shared,
In silent whispers, love is bared.
We rise anew, with grace we find,
The truth of hope, in hearts aligned.

Unyielding Faith

In whispers soft, His voice we hear,
A promise made, dispelling fear.
Through darkest nights, His light will shine,
In every trial, His love is mine.

With open hearts, we hold the flame,
For in our doubt, He calls our name.
Unyielding faith, a fortress strong,
In Him we thrive, where we belong.

A Beacon in the Storm

When raging seas seek to consume,
His presence comes, dispelling gloom.
As thunder roars and shadows creep,
He guides our souls, His watch we keep.

In every wave, His grace we find,
Our anchor firm, our hearts entwined.
A beacon bright, amidst the night,
In faith we stand, towards the light.

Where Hope Takes Root

In barren lands, a seed is sown,
With whispered dreams, new life is grown.
Through trials faced, our spirits soar,
In every heart, hope's gentle door.

With morning sun, our fears release,
In faith we gather, finding peace.
Where love abounds, and joy renews,
In every heart, hope's song ensues.

Illuminate the Unseen

In shadows deep where silence lies,
Your light, O Lord, ignites the skies.
With humble hearts, we seek the flame,
To guide our steps and praise Your name.

Through trials faced and doubts embraced,
Your presence, Lord, cannot be replaced.
In whispered prayers, we grasp the vine,
Our souls entwined, we feel divine.

The veils of night begin to part,
As faith ignites within the heart.
With every breath, we draw You near,
In every pulse, we feel You here.

O gentle breeze, Your love, we find,
In every leaf, in every kind.
Lead us forth with courage bold,
To share the light, to break the mold.

So let our spirits rise and soar,
In unity, we seek You more.
Illuminate the path we tread,
With hearts on fire, by hope we're led.

Heartstrings of Hope

In the still morning, whispers flow,
A symphony of grace bestowed.
With each heartbeat, love's refrain,
A promise echoes through the rain.

In every tear, a story shared,
A tapestry of souls prepared.
Uplifted hands to skies above,
United by the strength of love.

Through valleys low and mountains high,
Your guiding hand, we testify.
In moments dark, You shine so bright,
Our compass true, our faith, our light.

With every dawn, new dreams arise,
Resilient hearts embrace the skies.
For in Your arms, we find our peace,
In hope's sweet hymn, our fears release.

So let us walk, unfazed by fear,
Hands intertwined, we draw You near.
In heartstrings tugging, life unfolds,
A melody of grace, retold.

In the Arms of Hope

In shadows deep, we find the light,
A whispered prayer, our souls ignite.
Through trials faced, we rise anew,
In faith we walk, our spirits true.

With open hands, we seek the dawn,
Where love remains, and fear is gone.
In every heart, a flame shall glow,
Held gently tight, in arms of hope.

A Prayer for Perseverance

In quiet strength, we lift our pleas,
For steadfast hearts that bend like trees.
Through storms that rage, our roots hold fast,
In grace we tread, our shadows cast.

With every step, we forge the way,
In faith we stand, come what may.
Let courage swell, as doubts subside,
In unity, we will abide.

The Peace of Endurance

In trials faced, we find our peace,
Through every struggle, sweet release.
With patience deep, our souls expand,
In love's embrace, together stand.

Let burdens bear, in faith's soft light,
Our hearts entwined, we face the night.
With every breath, we seek the calm,
In trials met, our spirits balm.

The Weight of Grace

Upon our hearts, so gentle laid,
The weight of grace, our fears then fade.
In love's soft touch, we find our way,
Through darkest nights, into the day.

Forgiveness flows, like rivers wide,
In soulful binds, we will confide.
With open hearts, we journey on,
In grace we rise, till fears are gone.

Faith's Unyielding Embrace

In shadows deep, where hope may fade,
A whispered prayer, in silence laid.
Each tear, a step toward skies so bright,
In faith we walk, through darkest night.

With every doubt, my heart will soar,
Through trials faced, I seek Him more.
His love, a beacon, forever near,
In faith's embrace, I cast my fear.

In the Midst of Trials

When storms arise and winds do howl,
I find my strength, my spirit growl.
For trials shape the heart and soul,
In every struggle, I am whole.

With grace unfurled, I face the test,
In God I trust, my soul at rest.
Each challenge met, each burden shared,
In trials' grip, my faith is bared.

My Anchor Holds

When doubts press in and shadows loom,
I cling to hope, dispel the gloom.
My anchor firm, in Christ I find,
A steady heart, a peaceful mind.

The waves may crash, but I won't sway,
For in His love, I'll find my way.
With every storm, He stands so near,
In every trial, dispelling fear.

Upon the Rock, I Stand Firm

Upon the rock, my faith is laid,
In shifting sands, I am not swayed.
His promises, my fortitude,
In trials faced, I find His mood.

When tempests roar, I will not flee,
For steadfast love resides in me.
With courage found in every stance,
Upon the rock, I learn to dance.

Grace in Moments of Silence

In silence deep, His voice I hear,
A gentle call to draw me near.
With grace poured forth like morning dew,
In quietude, my strength renew.

Each moment still, His presence sweet,
In solitude, my heart's retreat.
With gratefulness, my spirit sings,
In quiet grace, my soul takes wing.

Where Faith Meets Fear

In shadows deep, where troubles dwell,
Faith rises high, breaks every shell.
When doubt surrounds, I seek the light,
With every step, I win the fight.

In whispered prayers, my heart finds peace,
Embracing hope, my worries cease.
For in His hands, I'm safe and sound,
Where faith meets fear, love knows no bound.

I Find My Way

Through winding roads, I roam and seek,
A guiding hand, both firm and meek.
In moments dark, I pause and pray,
With every breath, I find my way.

The compass bold, His word my guide,
In trials faced, I will not hide.
For in His grace, I feel the sway,
A steady heart, I find my way.

The Shelter of Unwavering Hope

Beneath the storm, I find my rest,
In Him alone, I am so blessed.
Through raging winds, and thunder's cry,
In shelter found, my soul can fly.

The distant stars, they shine so bright,
Each one a mark of endless light.
Where hearts may tremble, hope won't fade,
In steadfast love, my fears allayed.

Embracing the Gift of Endurance

In every trial, strength does grow,
A gift bestowed, to learn, to know.
With each new dawn, I rise and stand,
Endurance born from His own hand.

The path may twist, the skies may weep,
Yet in His arms, my soul will leap.
Through pain and loss, I hold so tight,
Embracing grace, I find the light.

The Call of the Spirit

When silence reigns, I hear the call,
A gentle nudge that breaks the fall.
In deepest night, the Spirit's song,
Reminds me where I truly belong.

Through trials fierce, His presence near,
With every breath, I shed my fear.
In whispered winds, I find my peace,
The call of Spirit, sweet release.

Resounding in Times of Trouble

When storms arise, and hearts grow frail,
In faith I stand, I shall not fail.
The echoes loud, of love profound,
Resounding truth, a steady sound.

Through valleys low, His promise clear,
In every tear, He draws me near.
With courage strong, I'll boldly tread,
In times of trouble, I am led.

In the Depths of Despair, I Rise

In shadows deep, my heart does weep,
Yet hope ignites, my spirit leaps.
With every tear, a prayer ascends,
In trials faced, my strength transcends.

When darkness calls, I seek the light,
Faith holds my hand, through endless night.
Each whispered vow, a guiding star,
In brokenness, I'm never far.

From ashes borne, new wings I'll find,
Through whispered grace, I'm redefined.
In silent trust, through pain I soar,
For in despair, I'm loved much more.

Though storms may rage, I stand my ground,
In every loss, His love I've found.
With open heart, I choose to rise,
For in His arms, my spirit flies.

Spirit's Fire, Unquenchable Flame

In the still night, Your whispers call,
A flame of love, ignites us all.
With fervent heart, we seek the spark,
In every trial, we leave our mark.

Though winds may howl, and shadows creep,
Within our souls, the fire we keep.
With every breath, our voices sing,
Of light unbound, and hope we bring.

Through darkened paths, Your light will guide,
With faith ablaze, we will not hide.
In sacred trust, our spirits rise,
As passion's flame, we will not die.

Together bound, our hearts unite,
In joyous dance, we meet the light.
With hands uplifted, we claim the day,
In Spirit's fire, we find our way.

Graceful Roots in Tempest's Grip

When storms descend, and doubts arise,
In faithful soil, my spirit lies.
With graceful roots, I'll stand my ground,
In tempest's grip, true strength is found.

Though winds may break, and rain may fall,
I bend but do not break at all.
With every wave that crashes near,
I rise in grace, dismissing fear.

Through trials harsh, I seek the light,
From deepest pain, I find my might.
In sacred trust, the roots run deep,
From darkest nights, my heart will leap.

With love as water, I will grow,
In stormy skies, my spirit glows.
For when the tempest starts to fade,
I stand renewed, my fears outweighed.

The Quiet Strength of Devotion

In silence held, my heart does speak,
With whispered prayers, my soul is meek.
In gentle hands, I find my peace,
From chaos-bound, I seek release.

With every dawn, my spirit wakes,
In sacred space, the stillness breaks.
Through humble acts, love's grace is shown,
In quiet strength, His presence known.

Though trials come, and shadows loom,
In faithful trust, I sense His bloom.
With heart aligned, I walk the path,
In steadfast joy, I feel His wrath.

In devotion true, my spirit flows,
As petals soft, affection grows.
In every moment, I seek to bind,
With quiet strength, I love unconfined.

The Path of Steadfastness

In shadows deep, we walk with light,
With every step, our spirits bright.
Through trials fierce, our hearts remain,
In faith we trust, through joy and pain.

The winding road may test our will,
Yet love's embrace, it lingers still.
With each new dawn, our souls ignite,
In steadfast hope, we find our sight.

Each moment passed, a chance to grow,
In sisterhood and brotherhood flow.
For every tear, a lesson shared,
Together strong, we are prepared.

With humble hearts, we seek the way,
In every night, we pray for day.
With arms outstretched, we rise above,
Bound by the force of endless love.

In the Stillness, We Trust

In quiet moments, grace we find,
A gentle whisper, pure and kind.
The chaos fades, our hearts align,
In sacred peace, our souls entwine.

As waters still, our spirits soar,
In this embrace, we seek for more.
A silent prayer, a candle's glow,
In faith, our seeds of hope will grow.

Through every storm, we hold on tight,
In darkest hours, we seek the light.
Trust is the bridge that takes us far,
In stillness found, we come to par.

So let us pause, breathe in the grace,
With open hearts, we find our place.
Each heartbeat sings a lullaby,
In stillness deep, we learn to fly.

Anchored by Faith

In tides that rise and waves that crash,
We find our strength, our spirits flash.
With roots of love, we stand our ground,
In every heartbeat, grace is found.

Through storms that rage, our hearts stay free,
With faith as anchor, we'll always be.
The winds may howl, the skies may gray,
But in His love, we find our way.

Each challenge met with steadfast pride,
With arms held high, we shall abide.
Through every trial, we stand tall,
Anchored by faith, we'll never fall.

In unity, our voices rise,
A chorus sweet beneath the skies.
With patient hearts, we'll carry on,
In every dusk, we greet the dawn.

A Curtain of Grace

In moments bright, and shadows low,
A curtain falls, the seeds we sow.
Each thread a promise, a touch divine,
In grace's fold, our spirits shine.

With gentle hands, the heart will mend,
In trials faced, we shall transcend.
Through every tear, a story spun,
A tapestry of love begun.

The fabric of faith, woven tight,
In darkened woods, we seek the light.
With every breath, we find our place,
Within the warmth of boundless grace.

So let us walk, in harmony,
With hearts united, strong and free.
A curtain drawn, our hopes embraced,
In love we dwell, in joy, we're placed.

Clinging to Faith's Gentle Hand

In shadows deep, where doubt may creep,
I find Your light, a promise to keep.
Through trials faced, I stand so tall,
With faith's embrace, I will not fall.

In every tear, a prayer is sown,
Your whispered love, my heart has known.
With each step taken, I hold on tight,
To faith's sweet hand, my guiding light.

When burdens weigh and nights grow cold,
Your warmth surrounds, a love untold.
In quiet moments, You bring me peace,
From every struggle, my worries cease.

In joyous songs, my heart will sing,
For in Your grace, I find my wings.
Each day I rise, with hope anew,
In faith's embrace, I trust in You.

Through valleys low and mountains high,
I'll journey forth, with You nearby.
In clinging close, my spirit thrives,
In faith I stand, I am alive.

In Trials, I Am Made Whole

In troubled waters, I seek Your face,
With every challenge, I find my place.
Through trials fierce, Your hand I feel,
In anguish deep, You make me heal.

When tempests rage and fears arise,
You lift my heart to boundless skies.
In darkest nights, Your light shines clear,
In trials faced, I draw You near.

With every stumble, I rise again,
Your strength within, my truest gain.
Through every tear, I am reborn,
In trials faced, a love well-worn.

You teach me grace, through pain I learn,
In brokenness, my heart will yearn.
For through the fire, my spirit grows,
In trials faced, my faith now glows.

In whispers soft, You call my name,
Through every storm, I know the same.
For in each test, I find my role,
In trials lived, I am made whole.

Divine Fortitude

When darkness falls and shadows creep,
Our souls awake from restless sleep.
With fortitude, we rise anew,
In strength divine, we'll see it through.

With each step forward, faith as guide,
We trust in Him, our souls abide.
In every hardship, we rejoice,
For in the silence, He's our voice.

With courage bold, we face the strife,
In trials faced, we find our life.
His spirit flows through every vein,
Our joy restored, released from pain.

Although the path may twist and turn,
In every loss, we choose to learn.
Together strong, we'll brave the night,
With hearts ablaze, we seek the light.

In every battle, He's our shield,
With faith and love, our wounds are healed.
Divine fortitude shall be our song,
In His embrace, where we belong.

In Unity, We Flourish

In sacred space, together strong,
We gather 'round, where we belong.
With hearts united, visions clear,
In unity, we cast our fear.

Through every trial, hand in hand,
In love's embrace, we make our stand.
For in our bond, we find our way,
A faithful light that guides our stay.

With open hearts and minds so free,
We share the gifts, in harmony.
In every blessing, every song,
In unity, we all belong.

The tapestry of lives entwined,
A sacred weave, divinely designed.
Through every storm, we shall endure,
In faith and hope, together pure.

From many voices, one refrain,
In fellowship, we rise again.
In unity, our spirits soar,
Together strong, forevermore.

In Sacred Stillness, I Find Peace

In quiet moments, I seek grace,
The whispers of love, a warm embrace.
In sacred stillness, hearts align,
Where faith and trust in spirit shine.

Beneath the stars, I cast my plea,
A gentle soul, I long to be.
In the silence, blessings flow,
With every breath, my spirit grows.

The world may roar, but I stand firm,
In sacred spaces, I find my term.
Each prayer a step on tranquil streams,
In holy light, I weave my dreams.

Through trials faced and burdens shared,
I walk with hope, my heart laid bare.
In sacred stillness, truth unspun,
A journey met, yet just begun.

I rise anew with every dawn,
In faith's embrace, I carry on.
In moments still, I find release,
In sacred stillness, I find peace.

A Song of Resilience

In shadows deep, I lift my voice,
A song of strength, I must rejoice.
For every trial that comes my way,
Resilience blooms, come what may.

Through storms that rage and winds that bite,
I stand unwavering, seeking light.
With every setback, I learn to grow,
A steadfast heart, come high or low.

In whispered prayers, my spirit soars,
Each challenge faced, I open doors.
A melody sweet in hopes refrain,
Through faith and courage, I break the chain.

I am the dawn that follows night,
A beacon brave, a guiding light.
With every note, my heart will sing,
A song of resilience I shall bring.

The path is long, yet I remain,
With faith as fuel, I know no pain.
In harmony, my truth will rise,
A song of strength beneath the skies.

A Trust Built on Solace

In stillness found, my heart will rest,
With every worry, I feel Your jest.
A trust built strong, like ancient stone,
In Your embrace, I'm never alone.

When shadows loom and fears take flight,
I turn to You, my guiding light.
In whispered hopes, my spirit sings,
A trust in You, my soul takes wings.

For in the quiet, Your love I feel,
A gentle balm, my wounds to heal.
Through all the trials, I keep my gaze,
On solace sweet, in prayer I raise.

With open hands, I yield my will,
In trust renewed, my heart is still.
For every burden, You'll bear the load,
A trust built strong, on love bestowed.

In sacred moments, I find my peace,
In trust I stand, my fears release.
With face uplifted, I walk with grace,
A trust built strong, my sacred space.

Through the Storm, My Spirit Soars

When thunder rolls and skies turn gray,
In turmoil's grip, I find my way.
Your presence fierce, a shield I wear,
Through the storm, I sense Your care.

With each fierce wind, my faith takes flight,
In roaring waves, I seek Your light.
For in the tempest, I make my stand,
With courage bold, and faith so grand.

Though doubts may rise and fears may shout,
I stand on truth, and cast them out.
Through raging seas, my spirit glows,
For in the storm, my heart still knows.

With every squall, I trust and lean,
On promises vast, yet unseen.
In trials faced, my spirit flies,
Through the storm, my soul defies.

In darkest hours, I feel Your grace,
Through every trial, I find my place.
For in the storm, I am restored,
Through the storm, my spirit soars.

Unfaltering in Faith

In shadows deep, we stand so tall,
With steadfast hearts, we heed the call.
In trials fierce, we find our way,
God's guiding light will never sway.

Through storms that roar, we hold on tight,
A beacon bright, our souls in flight.
With whispers soft, His grace we seek,
In every tear, He makes us meek.

With prayers aligned, our spirits rise,
The heavens smile, our hopes the skies.
In every moment, blessed and bright,
In faith we stand, our hearts ignite.

Though mountains high may block our view,
With open hearts, there's naught we rue.
His love will guide our weary feet,
In every challenge, we'll not retreat.

In unison, oh Lord, we sing,
A sacred bond, in faith we cling.
Through every doubt, we strive to know,
In His embrace, our spirits glow.

The Heart's Unyielding Promise

In quiet whispers, vows are made,
A promise blooms, shall never fade.
With hands uplifted, hearts entwined,
In love's embrace, our souls aligned.

Through tempests strong and trials long,
The heart remains where it belongs.
With faith unshaken, we press on,
In every dusk, a break of dawn.

With gentle grace, He holds our fears,
In every joy, in every tear.
Together, we shall stand as one,
His light will guide us till we're done.

The sacred bond, forever true,
In every promise, love renew.
Unyielding hearts in sacred trust,
With God above, in Him we must.

From valleys low to mountains high,
In unity, our spirits fly.
With every heartbeat, every prayer,
The heart's promise, divinely rare.

Divine Fortitude

When darkness falls and shadows creep,
Our souls awake from restless sleep.
With fortitude, we rise anew,
In strength divine, we'll see it through.

With each step forward, faith as guide,
We trust in Him, our souls abide.
In every hardship, we rejoice,
For in the silence, He's our voice.

With courage bold, we face the strife,
In trials faced, we find our life.
His spirit flows through every vein,
Our joy restored, released from pain.

Although the path may twist and turn,
In every loss, we choose to learn.
Together strong, we'll brave the night,
With hearts ablaze, we seek the light.

In every battle, He's our shield,
With faith and love, our wounds are healed.
Divine fortitude shall be our song,
In His embrace, where we belong.

In Unity, We Flourish

In sacred space, together strong,
We gather 'round, where we belong.
With hearts united, visions clear,
In unity, we cast our fear.

Through every trial, hand in hand,
In love's embrace, we make our stand.
For in our bond, we find our way,
A faithful light that guides our stay.

With open hearts and minds so free,
We share the gifts, in harmony.
In every blessing, every song,
In unity, we all belong.

The tapestry of lives entwined,
A sacred weave, divinely designed.
Through every storm, we shall endure,
In faith and hope, together pure.

From many voices, one refrain,
In fellowship, we rise again.
In unity, our spirits soar,
Together strong, forevermore.

In Sacred Stillness, I Find Peace

In quiet moments, I seek grace,
The whispers of love, a warm embrace.
In sacred stillness, hearts align,
Where faith and trust in spirit shine.

Beneath the stars, I cast my plea,
A gentle soul, I long to be.
In the silence, blessings flow,
With every breath, my spirit grows.

The world may roar, but I stand firm,
In sacred spaces, I find my term.
Each prayer a step on tranquil streams,
In holy light, I weave my dreams.

Through trials faced and burdens shared,
I walk with hope, my heart laid bare.
In sacred stillness, truth unspun,
A journey met, yet just begun.

I rise anew with every dawn,
In faith's embrace, I carry on.
In moments still, I find release,
In sacred stillness, I find peace.

A Song of Resilience

In shadows deep, I lift my voice,
A song of strength, I must rejoice.
For every trial that comes my way,
Resilience blooms, come what may.

Through storms that rage and winds that bite,
I stand unwavering, seeking light.
With every setback, I learn to grow,
A steadfast heart, come high or low.

In whispered prayers, my spirit soars,
Each challenge faced, I open doors.
A melody sweet in hopes refrain,
Through faith and courage, I break the chain.

I am the dawn that follows night,
A beacon brave, a guiding light.
With every note, my heart will sing,
A song of resilience I shall bring.

The path is long, yet I remain,
With faith as fuel, I know no pain.
In harmony, my truth will rise,
A song of strength beneath the skies.

Beneath the Weight, Hope Blossoms

Amidst the burden, shadows cling,
Yet in the heart, hope dares to spring.
Beneath the weight of doubt and fear,
A flower blooms, its path is clear.

In silent nights, when courage wanes,
I gather strength through gentle rains.
Each tear I shed, a seed I sow,
In every heartache, love will grow.

Through trials faced, I find my way,
With every dawn, a brighter day.
Beneath the weight, I stand up tall,
For hope is there to catch the fall.

In nature's arms, my spirit thrives,
Among the roots, true life derives.
With every breath, I choose to trust,
For blooming hope is my great must.

Beneath the weight, I walk anew,
A testament to all that's true.
In every challenge, I will see,
That hope, once sparked, will set me free.

The Path Less Traveled Is My Guide

In wanderings rare, I hear the call,
The path less traveled, I embrace it all.
With every turn, adventure's near,
In faith, I step beyond my fear.

The road is rough, yet beauty hides,
In challenges faced, my spirit bides.
With every trail, a lesson learned,
In every heart, a passion burned.

No map to follow, just steps divine,
In silent gazes, the stars align.
The path I tread is filled with light,
An inward journey, bringing sight.

I journey forth where few have gone,
In whispered truths, my heart is drawn.
With every heartbeat, I will strive,
For in this path, my soul's alive.

The road may wind, yet I am free,
In sacred trust, I walk with glee.
The path less traveled leads me home,
In every step, with love, I roam.

Sacred Moments of Resolve

In the silence, hearts align,
Whispers of faith intertwine.
Each breath a prayer, softly said,
In sacred moments, doubts are shed.

With every tear, a strength is found,
Through trials faced, in light we're bound.
A journey carved in trust and grace,
Our spirits soar, we find our place.

In unity, our voices rise,
A chorus strong beneath the skies.
With hands held high, we stand as one,
Through struggles faced, our hearts have won.

When shadows creep and fears abound,
We seek the light, on solid ground.
Each challenge met, with courage bold,
Together, we turn fears to gold.

In faith, we march, our purpose clear,
With love and hope, we conquer fear.
Forever bound by resolve's embrace,
In sacred moments, we find grace.

Together in Reverence

In the dawn's light, we gather near,
Hearts united, casting out fear.
In every prayer, a bond so tight,
Together we stand, embraced by light.

Through songs of praise, our spirits soar,
Each voice a beacon, forevermore.
With reverence deep, we seek the divine,
In sacred connection, our souls entwine.

With open hands, we share our plight,
Guiding each other through the night.
In moments of doubt, we find our strength,
Together in reverence, we go the length.

In silence shared, a knowing glance,
Through trials faced, we take our chance.
With faith as our shield, we journey on,
Together we rise, in the breaking dawn.

As echoes of love fill this place,
We celebrate life, in heartfelt grace.
In every breath, a promise made,
Together in reverence, we will not fade.

The Fortitude of Belief

In whispered prayers, we find our way,
Through darkest nights, into the day.
With every step, we forge ahead,
The fortitude of belief we spread.

In trials faced, we stand up tall,
With faith unyielding, we will not fall.
Each struggle met, a lesson learned,
In the fire of hope, our spirits burned.

From ashes rise, our purpose clear,
With love and strength, we conquer fear.
In unity's name, we press along,
Together we flourish, forever strong.

With open hearts, we share our light,
In the darkest hours, we are the bright.
Fortified by faith, we journey through,
In every heartbeat, the truth shines through.

As mountains move and rivers flow,
The fortitude of belief will grow.
In every challenge, we stand as one,
With hearts ablaze, we have just begun.

Through Shadows and Light

In shadows cast, we search for grace,
Through trials faced, we find our place.
With open hearts, we seek the way,
Through shadows and light, we cherish the day.

Each whispered prayer, a guiding star,
In moments of doubt, we've come so far.
With every step, we feel the soul,
Through shadows and light, we become whole.

In storms that rage, we hold on tight,
The strength of love, our heart's delight.
With faith beside us, we rise and shine,
Through shadows and light, our spirits entwine.

With unity forged in trials faced,
We find our purpose; our fears replaced.
In the tapestry of life, we weave,
Through shadows and light, we truly believe.

From darkness blooms a brilliant dawn,
In every heartbeat, we carry on.
Through shadows and light, we make our stand,
With open hearts, we'll heal this land.

Courage Under Heaven

When the storm clouds loom above,
We stand with hearts all aflame.
For in His light, we find our strength,
To rise above the fear and shame.

In whispers soft, He calls our name,
With love that never sways or wanes.
With courage found in faithfulness,
We face the trials, bear the pains.

His hope, a beacon shining bright,
Guides us through the darkest night.
With every step, we trust His plan,
Holding fast to His sacred might.

Like eagles soaring through the skies,
We spread our wings, embracing grace.
In unity, our spirits shine,
As we reflect His holy face.

Through valleys deep, we walk with trust,
In every heartbeat, prayers arise.
For courage lives within our souls,
With God, we conquer every rise.

Trusting Through Temptation

In shadows cast by whispered lies,
We find the strength to break away.
With faith as anchor, hearts aflame,
We seek His light to guide the way.

Though trials pull at weary souls,
And doubts may creep like silent night,
We stand in grace, unwavering,
Trusting Him to make all right.

The serpent's charm may lead us near,
With golden dreams and fleeting fame.
But truth unveils what's truly real,
And in His name, we stake our claim.

In every moment, choose the path,
That leads us back to love divine.
With wisdom won through prayer and time,
We'll rise above the fray, we shine.

So let the world throw wide its doors,
We stand as one, as heaven's kin.
With steadfast hearts and faith alive,
In Him, we find our strength within.

Cherished Through the Fire

In trials fierce, we are refined,
Like gold that shines from heat and flame.
For in the fire, we find our worth,
And learn to trust His holy name.

With every spark, He forms our hearts,
In patience, we embrace the test.
Each moment crafted by His grace,
Produces hope, our spirit's rest.

Though flames may dance around our feet,
We stand secure, unyielding, strong.
For He who forged us in the blaze,
Is faithful, loving, and belongs.

We bear the scars of battles fought,
Yet in each wound, His love we find.
For through the pain, we learn to see,
The beauty in His plans enshrined.

And when the ashes rest our feet,
We rise renewed, with purpose clear.
Cherished through every trial faced,
In His embrace, we cast out fear.

The Sanctuary Within

Deep in our hearts, a refuge lies,
A sacred space where faith abides.
Within the storms of life we face,
We find His love, where hope presides.

This sanctuary, built on prayer,
Supports our weary, fragile souls.
With every prayer, the walls grow strong,
His presence whispers, makes us whole.

As stillness wraps around our minds,
We feel His peace, a gentle balm.
In moments fraught with doubt and fear,
His light our guiding star, our calm.

Together in this hallowed ground,
We gather strength from those we love.
In unity, our spirits rise,
A testament to grace from above.

So let us dwell within this place,
Where sorrows fade and joy can reign.
The sanctuary, ever near,
In Him, we lose and find our gain.

A Journey of the Soul

In the quiet of the night,
I seek the path of light.
With each step, I find my pace,
Guided by a sacred grace.

Winds of change whisper near,
Carrying prayers, soft and clear.
Through valleys deep and hills that rise,
I search for truth beyond the skies.

Mountains echo with my cries,
As I reach for heaven's prize.
In every shadow, hope shines bright,
Illuminating darkest night.

Fellow travelers by my side,
Together in faith, we abide.
With each heartbeat, love does soar,
Binding souls forevermore.

Through the trials, we stay whole,
Each challenge deepens the soul.
A journey that never ends,
In light and love, we make amends.

Whispers of the Divine

In the silence, whispers flow,
With each breath, I come to know.
The gentle touch of grace divine,
In every heart, a sacred sign.

Stars above like stories writ,
Each one speaks of love's great fit.
The moonlight graces tranquil seas,
Carrying forth celestial pleas.

In the stillness, spirits sing,
Songs of hope and joy they bring.
Each note a promise, pure and bright,
Guiding souls through darkest night.

Nature blooms with vibrant hues,
In every petal, love imbues.
The trees, they dance, the winds embrace,
All creation sings His grace.

Through life's maze, we seek and strive,
For in this search, our dreams alive.
Whispers of the divine call clear,
In every moment, He is near.

Standing Together in Grace

In the circle of our trust,
Together we rise, as we must.
Hands held high, we lift each other,
As sisters and brothers, we discover.

Through trials and testings, we stand tall,
In unity, we conquer all.
Each heartbeat echoes the divine,
A tapestry of love we intertwine.

With hearts open to the skies,
We share our hopes, we share our cries.
In every struggle, joy we sow,
Together, side by side, we grow.

The grace that binds us, a sacred thread,
In every word of love we've said.
Through laughter's light and sorrow's tear,
In grace, we find our purpose here.

Let our voices rise in song,
In harmony, we all belong.
With every step, in faith we pace,
Forever standing here in grace.

Seeds of Faith in the Heart

In the garden of the soul,
Faith's soft whispers make us whole.
Planting seeds of love and trust,
In richness deep, we find our dust.

With nurturing hands, we watch them grow,
Through storms and sun, their strength will show.
Each bloom a testament divine,
In every petal, His light will shine.

The roots are strong, entwined with grace,
In every shadow, we'll find His face.
Together we flourish, hand in hand,
As we walk through this holy land.

Through seasons change, we rise and fall,
In every struggle, we hear His call.
With patience deep, we wait and pray,
For faith will guide us all the way.

So gather close, in joy's embrace,
With every smile, we see His face.
In hearts aglow, let love impart,
The sacred seeds of faith, our heart.

In This Sacred Journey, I Remain

In this sacred journey, I walk so bold,
Seeking the truth that the ancients told.
With every whisper, my spirit soars high,
Under the gaze of the eternal sky.

Guided by light that shines from within,
I embrace the grace that erases my sin.
Through valleys of doubt, I find my way,
Knowing the dawn will follow each fray.

A heart filled with love, a mind set on peace,
In the quiet moments, I find my release.
Strengthened by faith, I rise through the night,
Every step forward, a testament of light.

In temples of silence, I kneel and pray,
Grateful for blessings that never decay.
With each gentle breath, I reconnect deep,
In this sacred journey, my soul shall keep.

With Every Step, My Heart Is Steeled

With every step, my heart is steeled,
In trials and triumphs, my fate revealed.
The path that unfolds is divinely cast,
A journey of faith, from future to past.

With eyes on the horizon, I carry my cross,
Knowing each struggle is never a loss.
In shadows of anguish, I find the light,
For hope is a beacon, forever in sight.

The winds of change may howl and roar,
Yet I stand firm, my spirit shall soar.
In moments of doubt, I seek to believe,
For in faith's embrace, we truly receive.

Each stride that I take is a dance with grace,
In the tapestry woven, I find my place.
Surrounded by love, in the depths of my soul,
With every step, I am becoming whole.

In the Stillness, Courage Awaits

In the stillness, courage awaits,
Beneath the surface, where silence resonates.
With hearts intertwined, we gather to pray,
In the arms of the night, we find our way.

From whispers of doubt, to echoes of hope,
We walk hand in hand, learning to cope.
In the quiet embrace of a starry sky,
Our spirits are lifted, together we fly.

The stillness speaks volumes, a language divine,
In moments of stillness, our fears intertwine.
Though darkness may stretch like shadows at dusk,
In the depth of our souls, there lies a trust.

Awakened by peace, we rise once again,
To carry the light that will shine through the pain.
In the depths of our being, we foster our fate,
In the stillness, courage awaits.

Blessed Is the Path of Patience

Blessed is the path of patience divine,
Where whispers of wisdom in silence align.
With each gentle step, we nurture the earth,
Crafting our dreams, giving each seed its birth.

In waiting, I learn the gift of the pause,
As time weaves its magic, revealing the cause.
With faith as my compass, I walk with grace,
Embracing the journey, each moment I face.

Though trials may rise like mountains so steep,
In the heart of the struggle, my promise I keep.
Patience is woven in the fabric of time,
A testament of trust, a melody in rhyme.

Holding the light through the darkest of nights,
I find peace in the stillness, the softest of sights.
For blessed is the path where patience sows,
In gardens of grace, a true spirit grows.

So I walk forth with love, in every refrain,
Knowing each moment is never in vain.
With open arms, I welcome the day,
For blessed is the path, come what may.

Through the Valley, I Persist

Through the valley, I walk with grace,
Hand in hand with faith's embrace.
In moments dark, I find my way,
For in His light, I choose to stay.

Mountains loom, and shadows cast,
But I will stand, my fears outclassed.
With every step, I gain my strength,
Through trials faced, I'll go the length.

Whispers of doubt may fill the air,
Yet in my heart, a fervent prayer.
With steadfast mind, I journey on,
Trusting that love will carry dawn.

He leads me forth, a gentle guide,
In His embrace, I shall abide.
Though storms may rage and thunder call,
I find my peace, I will not fall.

So through the valley, I persist,
In every moment, His love exists.
With open heart and spirit free,
I walk with hope, eternally.

Steadfast Heart, Endless Light

In the quiet of the night,
My heart beats with endless light.
Through trials fierce, I hold my ground,
In sacred whispers, truth is found.

With every tear, a lesson learned,
In faith's embrace, my spirit burned.
A steadfast heart shall never wane,
In love divine, I rise again.

Guided by the stars above,
I carry forth a heart of love.
For in the dark, His face I find,
A beacon true, forever kind.

Each step I take, a prayer I weave,
With humble heart, I take my leave.
No fear shall grip, no doubt shall stand,
For I am safe within His hand.

So let the light within me shine,
A testament of love divine.
In every breath, I know my plight,
As steadfast heart meets endless light.

When Shadows Fall, Hope Remains

When shadows fall and hope seems lost,
I rise again, no matter the cost.
Through bitter nights, I seek the dawn,
For in His love, I am reborn.

The world may shake and tempests roar,
Yet through it all, I trust and soar.
With open arms, I greet the fight,
For in the dark, I hold His light.

Each moment filled with whispered grace,
A sacred bond that none can replace.
Through valleys deep and mountains high,
I lift my gaze and spread my wings to fly.

In every sorrow, there blooms a seed,
A testament to the heart's deep need.
For every trial shapes my soul,
And through His love, I am made whole.

So when shadows fall, I shall remain,
In steadfast hope, I'll bear the strain.
With faith as armor, I will stand,
Embraced forever by His hand.

Endurance Forged in Prayer

In quiet hours, my spirit sighs,
With every prayer, my soul will rise.
Through every storm, I seek His face,
A refuge found in boundless grace.

Each whispered word, a lifeline thrown,
In darkest nights, I'm never alone.
Through trials fierce, I learn to trust,
In faith's embrace, I am robust.

Forged in silence, my strength renews,
With love as fire, I won't refuse.
A heart resilient, a spirit brave,
In every moment, His peace I crave.

Through battles fought and lessons learned,
In steadfast hope, my heart has yearned.
For every prayer, a light that glows,
In endless cycles, love bestows.

So here I stand, a witness true,
Endurance built on faith anew.
With open heart, I rise and soar,
For in His love, I'm evermore.

The Promise of Tomorrow

In the quiet dawn, a whisper grows,
Hope like a river, boundless flows.
Each sun that rises, a gift anew,
A promise that life will guide us through.

In shadows cast by doubt's dark hand,
We stand together, strong we stand.
Faith lights the path where fear may tread,
With every step, our hearts are fed.

The skies may cloud and storms may rage,
Yet love will hold us, page by page.
Trust in the light that beckons near,
For tomorrow's dawn will chase all fear.

With every breath, we choose to sing,
Rejoicing in the joy He brings.
In valleys low and mountains high,
The promise of tomorrow will not die.

So lift your eyes to the endless skies,
Embrace the hope and let it rise.
For in each moment, grace will show,
The promise shines, let love bestow.

An Unshaken Spirit

In storms of life, my heart remains,
An anchor deep, through all my pains.
With faith unshaken, I stand my ground,
In His embrace, my peace is found.

The winds may howl, the waves may crash,
Yet in His presence, doubts will pass.
With each new trial that I face,
I find my strength in His pure grace.

The darkness falls, but I won't fear,
For in His light, I draw so near.
With steadfast heart and open mind,
In every struggle, hope I find.

In silence deep, His voice I hear,
Whispering truths that calm my fear.
An unshaken spirit, firm and bright,
Guided by faith, I'll walk in light.

With every heartbeat, I will soar,
On wings of love, forever more.
In all my journeys, come what may,
My spirit remains, unshaken, I pray.

Patience Born of Grace

In quiet moments, patience grows,
With every breath, the Spirit flows.
To wait for answers, soft and true,
Is grace revealed in all we do.

The winds may howl, the time may stall,
Yet in His arms, I will not fall.
For grace is there, a gentle guide,
A blooming flower that won't subside.

Each obstacle a lesson learned,
With every flicker, hope is burned.
In trials faced, a chance to see,
The beauty in the wait for me.

With heart so open, I shall trust,
In every moment, grace is just.
The waiting grounds me, keeps me whole,
In patience, I find my aching soul.

So in the dawn, when shadows creep,
In gentle whispers, I will keep.
Patience born of grace shall lead,
A steadfast heart in every need.

Perseverance Through Prayer

In whispered hopes, my heart takes flight,
Through every prayer, I seek the light.
With steadfast faith, I raise my plea,
In every moment, He walks with me.

Though trials come and shadows loom,
With prayerful whispers, I find my room.
A sacred space where I connect,
To draw the strength that I should not neglect.

Through valleys deep and mountains high,
With prayer I lift my spirit nigh.
In every tear, in every sigh,
My soul finds refuge, for He is nigh.

With every word, I find my way,
In faith renewed, I will not sway.
For perseverance blooms in grace,
As I abide in His embrace.

So let my heart be still and bright,
In every moment, trust the light.
Through prayer and hope, I'll always stand,
Perseverance strong, held in His hand.

The Light That Persists

In darkest nights, a whisper calls,
Hope shines bright when shadow falls.
Divine radiance pierces the gloom,
The promise of dawn dispels all doom.

Each heartbeat echoes with sacred grace,
In the stillness, we find our place.
Light eternal, steadfast and true,
Guiding the lost, revealing the due.

Through trials faced, we learn to see,
The ancient path that sets us free.
With every tear, a lesson dear,
Love's embrace casts away all fear.

When storms arise and doubts assail,
The spirit lifts with every wail.
For in the struggle, we find our might,
In the depths of pain, we grasp the light.

As seasons change and shadows wane,
We walk together through joy and pain.
In faith we stand, united and strong,
The light that persists will lead us along.

Through Trials We Rise

In the furnace of grief, we are forged,
With fire and faith, our spirits enlarged.
Though the weight of the world may bend the knee,
We learn to soar, we find our decree.

Each mountain climbed, a blessing bestowed,
Through valleys deep, our courage glowed.
In weariness, our hearts grow wise,
Through the stormy seas, together we rise.

With prayers whispered beneath the sky,
We gather strength as the days go by.
Hands held firm in times of strife,
Through trials we walk, embracing life.

From ashes of sorrow, new dreams will grow,
In sacred silence, love's river flows.
Through each challenge, faith ignites,
In united hearts, the spirit fights.

Together we lift, together we stand,
Guided by love, hand in hand.
Through trials faced, the truth unwinds,
In the rise of hope, a peace that binds.

Guided by Divine Hands

In every heartbeat, a whisper sweet,
Divine hands guiding, we're never discreet.
Through tangled paths and winding ways,
We walk in light through the darkest days.

The stars above, a celestial show,
Remind us gently that we are not alone.
With faith as our anchor, love as our guide,
In the arms of grace, we shall abide.

Each step we take, the spirits cheer,
In the journey ahead, we have no fear.
With open hearts, we embrace the call,
In humble surrender, we rise, we fall.

Through every trial, through each despair,
Divine hands lift us, an answered prayer.
In sacred unity, our souls will blend,
Together we'll soar, on wings we depend.

So let us dance in the light divine,
With every heartbeat, a sacred sign.
In the tapestry woven by love's embrace,
Guided by hands of infinite grace.

A Heart Unbroken

In the depths of struggle, a heart stands tall,
Resilient and steadfast, it answers the call.
When the world seems harsh and shadows loom,
A heart unbroken finds the bloom.

With whispers of hope in every sigh,
It learns to soar, to reach for the sky.
In adversity, lessons are sewn,
Each stitch a testament to seeds we've grown.

Through tears of sorrow and joy's sweet song,
A heart unbroken knows where it belongs.
It cradles love, embracing the pain,
Rising each time like sunshine through rain.

In moments of darkness, it shines ever bright,
Guided by faith, it knows wrong from right.
With compassion as armor, it stands so wide,
A heart unbroken, in love, it abides.

So let us cherish this gift we hold,
A heart unbroken, fierce and bold.
In unity, we shall find our way,
With love as our compass, come what may.

Rising Through the Ashes of Fear

In the valley of shadows, I stand tall,
With strength born anew, I heed the call.
From the embers of doubt, I rise each day,
Guided by faith, I find my way.

Each tear that has fallen, a lesson learned,
In the fire of trials, my spirit burned.
The ashes remind me of battles fought,
With courage ignited, all fear is sought.

As the dawn breaks free, dark nights recede,
Hope whispers softly, planting the seed.
With wings made of grace, my heart will soar,
Rising through ashes, I fear no more.

For deep in my soul, a promise shines bright,
That love will abound, illuminating the night.
In the garden of trust, my heart finds peace,
From the ashes of fear, my soul's release.

The Light Within That Never Fades

In the stillness of night, a candle glows,
A beacon of hope, where the spirit grows.
With whispers of angels, it calls my name,
Through darkness and doubt, it stays the same.

The storms may rage fierce, the winds may howl,
Yet deep within me, I hear Love's prowl.
A light in my heart, it ever remains,
Shining through trials, breaking the chains.

With every step taken, I journey on,
The road may be rocky, but I'm never alone.
For the light within me, a treasure bestowed,
Guides me through valleys where faith has flowed.

In moments of silence, I find the way,
The whisper of grace, my soul's gentle stay.
Through each fleeting hour, love's essence invades,
The light within me, it never fades.

My Waiting Is a Testament of Trust

In silence I linger, my heart beats slow,
Each moment a lesson, each breath a glow.
With hopes held high, I wait patiently,
For in the stillness, I'm learning to see.

Though patience be tested, my spirit stays strong,
In the hands of the Divine, I truly belong.
The promise of dawn, a whisper of grace,
In the depths of my waiting, I find my place.

In shadows and waiting, my faith is refined,
Trusting the journey, my heart intertwined.
With every heartbeat, my patience is blessed,
In the depth of my waiting, I find my rest.

For each tear that falls, a seed that I sow,
In the soil of trust, love's garden will grow.
My waiting is sacred, a pathway to light,
A testament of trust, ever shining bright.

Trials Shape the Heart of Gold

Through valleys of sorrow, the journey unfolds,
Where courage is tested, and soul's truth is told.
In the fires of trial, I find my worth,
For each struggle I face, rebirth from the earth.

Like the phoenix that rises, renewed from the flame,
Each challenge I conquer, I rise just the same.
In the forge of my trials, the heart learns to beat,
With rhythms of love, making life feel complete.

The beauty of struggle, a precious decree,
For trials are treasures, opening me.
In the heat of the moment, resilience grows bold,
As I learn through the trials, my heart becomes gold.

With faith as my anchor, I march through the storm,
Each challenge embraced, helps my spirit transform.
In the tapestry woven, my story is told,
In trials and triumphs, I shine like pure gold.

In the Shadow of the Almighty

In the shadow of the Lord, we find our peace,
With faith unyielding, our burdens cease.
His light surrounds us, a guiding star,
In every battle, He fights from afar.

In stillness, we hear His gentle call,
He lifts us up when we're ready to fall.
His refuge is mighty, our fortress strong,
In His embrace, we forever belong.

Through trials faced and storms that rage,
In Him, we write our sacred page.
His mercy flows like a river wide,
In the storm's eye, He stays by our side.

With every breath, we sing His praise,
In gratitude, our hearts ablaze.
He is the hope in a world of fear,
In the shadow of love, our path is clear.

Steadfast Souls

Steadfast souls in a world so vast,
Hold to the promises made in the past.
With hearts ablaze and spirits bound,
In unity, we rise from the ground.

Through trials faced, their faith shines bright,
Like stars that glimmer in the deepest night.
Guided by grace, their voices rise,
In every prayer, the faithful cries.

In the quiet moments, they seek His face,
For in His love, they find their place.
With every step, they boldly tread,
On paths of hope, where angels are led.

Their joy a beacon, their trust profound,
In the arms of the Savior, peace is found.
They carry burdens with grace and cheer,
Steadfast souls, forever near.

Rooted in Resilience

Rooted in resilience, we stand tall,
With faith like an oak, we will not fall.
Through storms that try to break our will,
We draw strength from the source that fills.

In trials faced, our roots grow deep,
In every hardship, His promises keep.
For every tear that we may shed,
He nurtures the life that blooms ahead.

Our spirits rise with every dawn,
In the light of hope, we carry on.
With hands uplifted and hearts sincere,
Rooted in love, we conquer fear.

Each challenge met, a lesson learned,
In the sacred fire, our hearts are burned.
From ashes of doubt, we find our voice,
Rooted in faith, we make our choice.

Anchored by Prayer

Anchored by prayer, we lift our gaze,
In whispered thoughts, our spirits raise.
In communion deep, our hearts align,
With every uttered word, His grace we find.

Through trials vast, we seek His face,
In moments of silence, we feel His embrace.
With every petition, our burdens share,
In the stillness of night, He's always there.

With hands clasped tight, we find our strength,
In faith, we journey a sacred length.
As seasons change and winds may blow,
Anchored by prayer, our roots will grow.

In the dance of life, we learn to trust,
With every step, in Him, we must.
For in the quiet, His peace descends,
Anchored by prayer, our journey mends.

A Journey Taken in Faith

With footsteps guided by His light,
We wander paths through the night.
Each moment filled with grace,
In faith, we find our sacred place.

The road may twist, the journey long,
Yet in our hearts, we hold the song.
A whisper calls, the Spirit near,
In trials faced, we cast out fear.

Through valleys deep and mountains high,
We raise our hands, we reach the sky.
In every step, His love shall lead,
In every heart, His truth we heed.

With every prayer, our spirits soar,
Through open doors, we seek Him more.
In communion, hopes do weave,
Together strong, we shall believe.

So here we stand, united true,
With hearts ablaze, His will we do.
A journey blessed, in faith we tread,
With light ahead, and love to spread.

Under the Gaze of Mercy

Beneath the shadow of His grace,
We find our tears, a warm embrace.
In silence deep, His heart reveals,
A love that mends, a warmth that heals.

The burdens heavy on our soul,
He lifts them high, He makes us whole.
In every trial, His mercy flows,
A river wide, where hope bestows.

With every sigh, we call His name,
In anguish faced, we feel the same.
Yet in the dark, a light ignites,
Illuminating our darkest nights.

In moments lost, when faith is weak,
He speaks to us, the words we seek.
A gentle nudge, a kind decree,
"Fear not, beloved, come unto Me."

So under gaze so pure and kind,
We shed our doubts, our hearts aligned.
In mercy's flow, forever blessed,
We find our peace, our souls at rest.

Hearts Whole in His Presence

In silence shared, we gather close,
With hearts that bloom, like sacred rose.
In every glance, His love we find,
A gentle touch that makes us blind.

Each moment spent in His sweet grace,
Transforms our lives, our sacred space.
In joy profound, we lift our song,
For in His arms, we all belong.

With hands uplifted, spirits rise,
In worship's glow, we touch the skies.
Together built, our faith entwined,
In unity, our hearts aligned.

No longer lost, no longer stray,
In His embrace, we live each day.
With hearts made whole, we stand anew,
In every breath, we feel Him true.

So come, dear friends, in love's embrace,
Together let us seek His face.
With hearts aflame, His light we share,
In presence pure, we find our prayer.

The Song of the Faithful

In melodies that rise like dawn,
We lift our voices, never gone.
A symphony of souls in grace,
Creating beauty, time and space.

Each note a prayer, a whisper sweet,
In harmony, our spirits meet.
With every chord, we stand as one,
In His name, our journey's begun.

From every trial, we carry forth,
A song of hope, a vibrant worth.
In joy and pain, our hearts will sing,
The love of Christ, our offering.

So let the echoes fill the air,
With every breath, we lift in prayer.
In gratitude, our song will flow,
For in His care, we surely grow.

Together in this sacred choir,
We sing of faith that won't expire.
With joyful hearts, let praises ring,
The song of the faithful, forever sing.

Holding on in Reverence

In the hush of morning's light,
We gather hope, hearts take flight.
Voices whisper, prayers ascend,
In reverence, we find our friend.

Faith like a candle, glowing bright,
Guides us through the darkest night.
With gentle hands and steadfast grace,
We hold on tight, in sacred space.

Each moment a gift, divinely bestowed,
On this path where love is sowed.
We bear the fruits of labored prayer,
In the garden of faith, we share.

Through trials faced and joys we sing,
In our hearts, the angels bring.
A symphony of trust and tears,
Holds us close through fleeting years.

So let us kneel, and hearts align,
In this sacred act, we shine.
Together we rise, inspire and mend,
Holding on in reverence, till the end.

The Silence of Belief's Strength

In the stillness, faith lays bare,
Whispers of hope fill the air.
Silent strength, a shroud we wear,
Guiding souls through every care.

Beneath the trials, spirits soar,
In quietude, we seek what's more.
Belief untouched by storms and strife,
Holds the promise of a new life.

When words grow heavy, silence speaks,
In sacred hush, our heart still seeks.
The essence of truth, a gentle breeze,
In this stillness, we find peace.

Awash in love, we intertwine,
Each moment sacred, nearly divine.
With quiet faith, our burdens lift,
In the silence, we find our gift.

Together we walk, in shadows dismissed,
With belief's strength, we can't resist.
In every silence, a voice of light,
Guides us gently through the night.

Embracing the Divine Path

On this journey, hearts entwined,
We seek the light that's long defined.
Footsteps tracing on sacred earth,
Embracing the path of rebirth.

Guided by love, we shed our fear,
In every breath, the divine draw near.
With open arms, we share our song,
A melody where all belong.

Through valleys deep and mountains wide,
Together we walk, side by side.
In every trial, we find the grace,
Embracing joy in this holy place.

Faith is our anchor, hope is the sail,
In storms of life, we shall not fail.
With hearts as one, we rise above,
Embracing the path, we walk in love.

As dawn breaks forth with colors fair,
We lift our voices to the air.
In every moment, a chance to grow,
Embracing the divine, let our hearts glow.

An Anthem of Perseverance

When shadows beckon, strength appears,
An anthem sung through countless tears.
With steadfast hearts, we break the chains,
Perseverance flows in our veins.

In trials faced with each new day,
We find a path, a brighter way.
With courage fierce and spirits bold,
We'll weather storms, our story told.

Through every struggle, we rise and stand,
With faith as our guide, united hand-in-hand.
Together we march, through thick and thin,
An anthem of hope, we hold within.

With every heartbeat, we cling to grace,
In the dance of life, we find our place.
An unwavering light, piercing the night,
An anthem of perseverance, shining bright.

So let the world hear our refrain,
In unity's bond, we shall remain.
Through trials and triumphs, we sing as one,
An anthem of life has just begun.

In Silence, We Stand

In quietude, we seek His face,
With humble hearts, we find our place.
Each whispered prayer, a sacred song,
In silence deep, we all belong.

Beneath the stars, His love displayed,
In shadows where our doubts did fade.
We gather here, our spirits rise,
In sacred trust, beneath the skies.

The stillness speaks, His voice so near,
In every tear, He wipes our fear.
With faith unbroken, we will stand,
Together bound by His holy hand.

In whispers soft, the truth is found,
In silence pure, our hearts unbound.
We walk the path He sets for us,
In quiet strength, we place our trust.

Our souls entwined in His embrace,
In silence, we find boundless grace.
With every breath, we sing His name,
In faith, united, we remain.

Unfading Love's Embrace

In morning light, we lift our gaze,
To unfading love that guides our ways.
With open hearts, we seek to learn,
In every moment, His light burns.

Through trials faced and storms we brave,
His love surrounds, it comforts, saves.
In darkest nights, we find our rest,
In His warm light, we are truly blessed.

Each step we take, His hands hold tight,
In love's embrace, we find our might.
No shadow deep can hide His grace,
In every trial, love takes its place.

From mountain high to valley low,
His love remains, our hearts will know.
Together we rise, our spirits soar,
In unity, His love restores.

In every heartbeat, His truth is clear,
A gentle whisper, forever near.
Unfading love, in Him we trust,
In faith and hope, our souls adjust.

Pillars of the Faithful

We stand as pillars, firm and strong,
In faith combined, we all belong.
With every prayer, our spirits soared,
In unity, His love restored.

With hands held high, we face our fears,
In every storm, He calms our tears.
Together bound, our voices raised,
In sacred truth, we lift our praise.

Each trial brings a chance to grow,
In love's embrace, our hearts will glow.
We walk in light, our paths aligned,
In faithful hearts, His peace we find.

The echo of our voices blend,
Together we are, until the end.
With every heartbeat, we declare,
In love and faith, we share His care.

As pillars strong, we shall not fall,
In every moment, we stand tall.
With faith unyielding, we press on,
In hope and love, we draw upon.

Everlasting Hope's Echo

In every heart, hope finds a spark,
In darkest nights, it leaves a mark.
With every dawn, new dreams arise,
Everlasting hope, our spirits prize.

We journey forth with open eyes,
In faith, we walk, through lows and highs.
The echo of His love resounds,
In every step, His grace abounds.

Through trials fierce, our spirits shine,
In every moment, love divine.
With open arms, we give our all,
In hope's embrace, we shall not fall.

The whispers soft, like gentle rain,
In every heart, He heals our pain.
With every breath, we cherish grace,
In hope's embrace, we find our place.

Everlasting hope, our guiding light,
In darkest days, it shines so bright.
Through love and faith, we stand as one,
In unity, our race is run.

Spirit of the Unbroken

In shadows deep, we rise anew,
With light of truth, we pierce the blue.
The spirit strong, it holds the key,
Unbroken hearts, forever free.

Through trials faced, we find our way,
In grace bestowed, we cease to fray.
Each whispered prayer, a guiding light,
The spirit shines through darkest night.

In unity, our voices blend,
A symphony where love transcends.
With faith that binds, we brave the storm,
Together strong, we will transform.

A tapestry of souls entwined,
In sacred love, we seek, we find.
The spirit calls, a gentle breeze,
An endless dance that never leaves.

So let us walk, hand in hand, true,
With hearts ablaze, in all we do.
For in this life, we shall be led,
By spirit's grace, we'll forge ahead.

Heartbeats of Faith

In every heartbeat, faith resides,
A sacred pulse that gently guides.
Through trials faced, we stand as one,
With hope that shines like morning sun.

In whispered prayers, the soul takes flight,
With every dawn, we chase the light.
Through valleys low and mountains high,
Our faith, a beacon in the sky.

Each breath we take, a promise made,
In love's embrace, no fear will fade.
Together bound, our spirits soar,
In heartbeats of faith, we trust evermore.

In quiet moments, we reflect,
The strength of faith that we protect.
Through storms that rage, we find our way,
In heartbeats of faith, we choose to stay.

So let us walk, with hearts ablaze,
In every moment, sing His praise.
United strong, in love we stand,
Heartbeats of faith across the land.

Through Belief We Stand

Through trials fierce, our spirits rise,
In whispered truths, we touch the skies.
With every step, on faith we tread,
Through belief we stand, our hearts are fed.

In unity, our voices sing,
A hymn of hope, the joy we bring.
Through storms of doubt, we hold the line,
In trust and love, our lives entwine.

With every shadow, light appears,
In sacred moments, calm our fears.
Through belief we stand, we gather strength,
A tapestry of faith, at length.

In every heart, a spark ignites,
In darkest hours, our love ignites.
Through trials faced, we will not part,
For in belief, we find our start.

So let us march, our hands held high,
With hearts ablaze, we touch the sky.
In every moment, let us strive,
Through belief we stand, forever alive.

The Calm in Our Tempest

When storms arise, and winds may howl,
We find our peace in sacred vow.
The calm within, our hearts embrace,
In waves of love, we find our place.

In shadows cast, we seek the light,
A guiding star, our hope shines bright.
With faith that steadies, fear departs,
The calm in tempest, love imparts.

In every trial, we find our way,
Through darkest nights, we seize the day.
With gentle whispers, grace surrounds,
In hearts united, peace abounds.

So when the world seems full of strife,
We turn to love, the source of life.
In every moment, trust will bloom,
The calm in our tempest, dispel the gloom.

Together strong, we face the storm,
In unity, our hearts transform.
With love as anchor, we will stand,
The calm in our tempest, hand in hand.

The Melody of Hope

In the stillness of the night,
A whisper calls the soul to rise,
With every heartbeat, hope ignites,
A symphony that never dies.

Through valleys low, we find our way,
With faith as guide, we shall not sway,
For every tear that grace bestows,
In trials faced, our strength still grows.

The dawn shall break, a brand new song,
In unity, we all belong,
With voices raised, we sing our part,
A melody that warms the heart.

The stars above, like dreams so bright,
Remind us of eternal light,
For in the dark, our spirits soar,
To hope and peace, we shall implore.

So let our hearts in rhythm beat,
With love and light, our lives complete,
In every note, a promise found,
The melody of hope resounds.

Abiding in His Love

In quiet moments, hearts entwine,
A sacred bond, forever shine,
Through trials faced, we find our peace,
In His embrace, our fears release.

His love, a river flowing wide,
With open arms, He's by our side,
No heights, no depths can keep apart,
The gentle whisper ofHis heart.

When shadows loom and doubts arise,
He shines His light, dispels our cries,
In every breath, His grace abound,
Through every path, His love is found.

With faith, we tread the road ahead,
In trust, His words, we daily spread,
Abiding in this love so true,
We find our strength in all we do.

In every moment, let us see,
The beauty of His love set free,
A tapestry of grace and hope,
In Him, we stand, we rise, we cope.

The Embrace of Resilience

Through storms that rage, we stand our ground,
With faith as our unshakeable sound,
Each trial faced, a lesson learned,
In every heart, the flame is burned.

Resilience blooms in desert sands,
In brokenness, a strength expands,
With every fall, we rise again,
In His arms, we shed our pain.

The path is steep, yet we press on,
With courage found, we greet the dawn,
In every challenge, hope restores,
Through open hearts, our spirit soars.

With every tear, we find our way,
For love will guide, come what may,
In every moment, faith avows,
The embrace of resilience empowers.

So let us journey, hand in hand,
With love and strength, united stand,
In every heartbeat, let us rise,
Embraced by grace, we claim the skies.

In His Light, We Remain

In shadows deep, His light will lead,
A gentle hand, our every need,
With grace abounding, peace will flow,
In His embrace, our spirits glow.

Through darkest nights, He shines so bright,
A beacon bold, our guiding light,
In every trial, love prevails,
In Him, our hope forever sails.

With faith renewed, we walk the way,
In trust, we rise with each new day,
His words ignite the flame of truth,
In every heart, He reigns with proof.

So let us stand in awe and praise,
In gratitude, our voices raise,
For in His light, we find our peace,
In His embrace, our fears release.

Together bound, our spirits soar,
In His love, we need not more,
With every step, His light remains,
In faith and hope, our joy sustained.

Eclipsed Yet Radiant

In shadows cast by doubts untold,
I seek the light, the truth to hold.
Though moments darken, faith remains,
His grace will guide through all my pains.

The sun may fade behind the night,
Yet in my soul, there burns a light.
Eclipsed, yet radiant, love will rise,
A beacon bright against the skies.

In trials faced, I stand my ground,
For in His arms, my peace is found.
When storms assail and shadows grow,
His whispers calm, my spirit's glow.

Through every tear, each silent prayer,
His presence soothes, I feel Him near.
In darkest hours, hope takes flight,
With faith as wings, I soar to light.

I walk this path, though steep and wide,
With steady heart and soul as guide.
For every step, His promise stays,
Each moment rich with sacred ways.

A Peace That Passes Understanding

In quiet moments, peace descends,
A gentle balm that softly mends.
When chaos reigns and troubles loom,
His love, a light in every room.

Like rivers flowing deep and clear,
His calming voice I long to hear.
When noise of life begins to swell,
I find in Him my restful well.

The world may shake, its heart may quake,
Yet in my spirit, joy won't break.
A peace that passes all I know,
Shines brightest in the depths of woe.

He holds the storms within His hand,
And guides my heart to solid land.
I walk with faith, though steps unsure,
With every breath, I feel Him near.

In every sigh, a trust I claim,
Through life's wild dance, I praise His name.
For in His arms, my soul takes flight,
And in His love, I find my light.

The Journey of Many Steps Uphill

Each step I take, a path unfolds,
In faith I walk, though fears be bold.
The climb is steep, the road is long,
Yet in my heart, I find a song.

I measure time by grace bestowed,
Through trials faced, my spirit glowed.
Each stumble teaches, every fall,
I rise again, I heed His call.

With every breath, my burdens lift,
He gives me strength, a holy gift.
Though weary bones may ache and tire,
His love ignites a blazing fire.

The journey winds through dark and light,
With weary heart, I seek the right.
His presence fills the air I breathe,
In every moment, I believe.

Through narrow paths and valleys wide,
I lean on Him, my faithful guide.
With every step, I find my way,
In joy and sorrow, I shall stay.

Through Gloom, My Heart Shall Sing

Though shadows linger, dark and deep,
My heart shall rise, no need for sleep.
In moments bleak, when hope seems lost,
I count the blessings, and the cost.

Through trials faced, my spirit's bright,
For in the gloom, I find the light.
With every tear, a song I weave,
Believing still, I shall believe.

Each storm that passes, clouds may part,
With every beat, I guard my heart.
His love will shine, a radiant beam,
Illuminating every dream.

Though dark may linger, dawn shall break,
And in the night, new hope I'll make.
Through every woe, my soul shall rise,
A melody that fills the skies.

So come what may, I choose to sing,
Through every challenge that life may bring.
For in the gloom, my heart takes flight,
Forever held in His pure light.

The Well of Steadfastness

In shadows deep, my spirit stands,
By faith I drink from sacred lands.
A well of truth, my soul it binds,
In quiet grace, my heart aligns.

With every trial, I find my way,
In whispered prayers that softly sway.
The waters cool, they soothe my strife,
In steadfastness, I find my life.

Through desert paths and jagged stones,
I walk with trust, my spirit grown.
The well within, so deep, so wide,
In stillness flows, my faithful guide.

From barren lands, the blossoms rise,
With every drop, a new surprise.
The well of strength, it never dries,
In every heart, a love that ties.

So bring your doubts, lay down your fears,
In the well's embrace, wipe away tears.
With steadfast hearts, we journey on,
Together in faith, till the break of dawn.

Carrying the Cross of Patience

In the weight of sorrow, hope is found,
As I carry my cross upon this ground.
Each step I take, with mercy's grace,
Unseen hands guide me through this space.

The thorns that prick, the burdens laid,
In patience, I stand, undismayed.
With every labor, a purpose blooms,
In trials faced, the spirit resumes.

From weary nights to brightening days,
With faith ablaze, I seek His ways.
An echo soft, a gentle call,
In patience learned, I conquer all.

In moments long, my heart grows still,
Embracing pain, fulfilling His will.
The cross I bear, a sacred trust,
Through valleys low, to heights of dust.

So let me walk, though heavy the load,
With patience strong, along His road.
For in the waiting, my soul will rise,
Transformed by love, beyond the skies.

Beneath the Wings of Hope

In gentle hush, the shadows fall,
Beneath His wings, I heed the call.
A refuge found from storms that rage,
In hope's embrace, I turn the page.

With every sigh, a prayer takes flight,
In darkness deep, I seek the light.
The wings of peace, they shelter me,
In whispered dreams, I long to be.

Through trials fierce, my heart takes wing,
In every note, a song to sing.
The dawn shall rise, the night must yield,
Beneath His wings, my heart is healed.

So lift your eyes to skies above,
In shadows cast, He weaves His love.
With open hearts, we rise and soar,
In hope's embrace, forevermore.

Together bound, in faith we gleam,
Beneath the wings, we live the dream.
In harmony, our spirits blend,
With hope that lasts, till journeys end.

The Tapestry of Strength

In threads of light, our stories wove,
The tapestry of strength, a gift from above.
Each color bright, each pattern true,
In every stitch, a faith anew.

From joy to pain, each moment sewn,
In unity's weave, we are never alone.
The fabric strong, it binds our hearts,
Through every trial, true beauty starts.

With every tear, a story shared,
In love's embrace, we are always prepared.
The tapestry grows, with hands entwined,
In strength we rise, our souls aligned.

So let us toil, with purpose keen,
In every thread, His love is seen.
The tapestry tells of paths we trod,
In strength found here, we honor God.

Together we stand, together we strive,
In the tapestry of life, we thrive.
With threads of faith, let us embrace,
The strength of love, our saving grace.

Whispers of Hope in the Darkened Night

In shadows deep, where silence dwells,
A gentle breeze of grace compels.
With every breath, the soul ignites,
Whispers of hope in the darkened nights.

The stars above, they softly gleam,
A reminder of a distant dream.
In prayerful heart, I find my way,
Guided by faith, to greet the day.

When trials loom and fears arise,
I seek the light beyond the skies.
With every tear, a promise sown,
In darkest hours, I am never alone.

The dawn will break, the shadows flee,
In every struggle, there You'll be.
With whispered strength, I find my peace,
In moments hard, my love won't cease.

So let me walk, both brave and free,
With every step, I trust in Thee.
For hope's sweet song shall ever ring,
Through darkened night, my heart will sing.

Climbing the Mountain of My Trials

The mountain looms, both tall and steep,
Each step I take, my faith run deep.
With weary legs, I climb anew,
Trusting the path that leads me through.

The rocks may slip, the winds may blow,
Yet in my heart, the strength will grow.
For every trial, a lesson learned,
With every struggle, my spirit burned.

I reach for light, though clouds may shade,
In every moment, my fears evade.
With prayers like anchors, I hold them tight,
Guided by love, I chase the light.

Each summit calls, a promise near,
Through pain and joy, my vision clear.
In every breath, a hope alive,
Climbing the mountains, I will survive.

So here I stand, no turning back,
With faith beside me, I'll stay on track.
For on this journey, I truly find,
The strength of heart and peace of mind.

Even When Broken, I Am Blessed

In shattered pieces, light can shine,
Even when broken, my heart aligns.
With every crack, the grace flows through,
In darkest days, I am made new.

The scars I wear tell tales profound,
Of battles fought, of grace unbound.
For every wound, a story's spun,
Of love that heals when the day is done.

In silence deep, I find my song,
Even when broken, I can be strong.
With gratitude, I lift my voice,
In every hurt, I still rejoice.

The blessings bloom from ashes cast,
In every trial, my faith holds fast.
For in my heart, the truth will rest,
Even when broken, I am blessed.

So let the storms arise and rage,
In gentle strength, I find my stage.
With every breath, I embrace the light,
Even when broken, I walk in grace bright.

Bound by Love, Unshaken I Stand

In bonds of love, my heart is tied,
Through storms that rage, I will abide.
With faith as my anchor, strong and true,
Bound by love, I will see it through.

When shadows fall and doubts arise,
I lift my gaze towards the skies.
For in His arms, I find my rest,
In trials faced, I am truly blessed.

With every heartbeat, His grace flows free,
Guiding my steps, surrounding me.
Through every fall and every rise,
I find my strength in love's great ties.

In unity, we face the night,
With hope ablaze, we seek the light.
Together, hand in hand, we stand,
Bound by love, unshaken I stand.

With every breath, my spirit sings,
For in His love, my heart takes wings.
Through trials fierce, my truth is found,
In love's embrace, forever bound.

Resilience in Reverence

In the shadow of the storm, we stand,
With hands uplifted, we seek Your hand.
Among the trials, we find our grace,
In every challenge, we see Your face.

Hearts entwined with hope's embrace,
Through every struggle, we find our place.
In whispers soft, Your truth resounds,
With each beat, our faith abounds.

When the world seems heavy and worn,
In quietude, our spirits are born.
From ashes rise, the soul ignites,
In reverence, we claim our rights.

With courage found in sacred time,
We walk the path, and we climb.
In every moment, strength displayed,
With hearts adorned, our fears allayed.

Together we stand, in dawn's first light,
With hope unyielding, spirits bright.
In love's embrace, we rise anew,
For in Your presence, we are true.

Courage in Quietude

In stillness, a whisper, the heart's true call,
A strength so quiet, yet never small.
Hands clasped in prayer, eyes softly closed,
In sacred silence, our courage grows.

Through valleys low, through mountains high,
With faith unbroken, we learn to fly.
Each breath a testament, a vow we make,
In life's sweet dance, there's more at stake.

When shadows linger, and doubts arise,
In the quietude, our spirit flies.
For in these moments, we see the truth,
Embedded brightly in the hands of youth.

With hearts aligned, we face the day,
In every challenge, we find our way.
Together we journey, hand in hand,
A testament to the love that's grand.

From softest whispers, courage springs,
In faith's embrace, the heartache stings.
And so, in quietude, we take our stand,
With the strength of the Almighty at our command.

Faith's Firm Foundation

Upon the rock, our faith will stand,
A fortress built by His own hand.
When storms do rage, and darkness falls,
In Your embrace, our spirit calls.

Each stone a prayer, each breath a song,
In Your love, we truly belong.
Through trials faced, we stand our ground,
In faith's firm light, our strength is found.

The path may twist, but we shall not sway,
Your guiding light will show the way.
In every heartbeat, a promise sealed,
With faith unshakeable, our fates revealed.

With hands of grace, we build anew,
With every challenge, a stronger view.
In every dawn, Your mercy shines,
A testament to love divine.

Together we rise, united we stand,
In faith's firm bond, hand in hand.
For in Your truth, we find our way,
A beacon bright, come what may.

Through Darkness, We Shine

In darkest nights, we find the glow,
A light that whispers, a love we know.
With faith as our lantern, we boldly tread,
Carrying hope where shadows spread.

For in the silence of the gloom,
Bright blooms of courage begin to loom.
In every heartbeat, a sacred spark,
We illuminate paths in spaces dark.

Through trials faced, our spirits soar,
In the arms of love, we long for more.
With eyes wide open, we seek and find,
The glimmering gifts left behind.

In every tear, a story spun,
In every moment, we are one.
Through valleys deep and mountains steep,
Our faith ignites, our promises keep.

Together we lift, together we rise,
In the face of despair, we claim the skies.
For through the darkness, our love defines,
An unwavering flame, through trials, we shine.

The Celestial Call of Resilience

In the silence, I hear Your grace,
A whisper calling through time and space.
With faith as a shield, I rise anew,
Guided by light, I journey through.

Mountains may tremble, storms may roar,
Yet in Your arms, I stand in awe.
Each setback a step to greater heights,
For Your love ignites my inner lights.

The wounds I bear, they start to heal,
With every prayer, I know You're real.
A tapestry woven with pain and glee,
Your presence, Lord, sets my spirit free.

Through shadows deep and valleys wide,
I walk with You, my faithful guide.
With every heartbeat, my strength is clear,
In trials faced, I feel You near.

In the celestial call, I find my way,
Resilience blooms with each passing day.
With trust unshaken, I stand tall,
Forever anchored in Your love's call.

Enduring Through His Embrace

In every storm, I seek Your face,
A gentle warmth, my sacred space.
Your arms, a refuge from the fight,
In darkness, Lord, You are my light.

Through trials faced, my spirit bends,
Yet in Your love, my heart transcends.
Each day I rise, anew, renewed,
By grace unearned, my faith pursued.

You gather tears and hold them tight,
Transforming sorrow into light.
With every step, I hear Your name,
A beacon shining, always the same.

In valleys low, You walk beside,
With whispered truths, my fears subside.
Embraced in hope, I forge ahead,
For in Your glory, I am led.

Through trials faced, I shall not part,
Enduring love within my heart.
With every breath, I choose to sing,
In His embrace, my soul takes wing.

The Spirit's Unyielding Song

In silent nights, the spirit sings,
A melody of hope that clings.
It dances through the darkest times,
A sacred rhythm, love that rhymes.

Each note a prayer, a whispered plea,
Carved in the heart, forever free.
In anguished cries, Your peace I find,
With every hymn, my soul aligned.

The trials faced like shadows flee,
Your grace, my guide, will always be.
In valleys deep or mountains high,
I feel the strength of wings to fly.

The spirit's song, a sacred thread,
In every tear, the joy instead.
With every heartbeat, I declare,
In faith unfaltering, I lay bare.

In unyielding love, I stand and know,
Your spirit's song will ever flow.
Together, Lord, we rise and soar,
In harmony, forevermore.

When Trials Lead to Triumph

In shadows cast, I see the light,
When trials loom, I stand in fight.
Each challenge faced, a lesson learned,
In hardship's fire, my spirit burned.

With faith as my compass, I forge ahead,
Through tempest's roar, where angels tread.
Your promise whispers in the night,
A guiding star, unyielding bright.

Though valleys steep may draw me low,
Your hand, O Lord, will help me grow.
In every trial, I find my way,
From ashes rise to greet the day.

Each wound and scar, a story told,
In love's embrace, my heart is bold.
With every breath, a victory claimed,
When trials pass, my soul unchained.

From brokenness to strength I rise,
In triumph's glow, my spirit flies.
For in Your grace, I stand refined,
When trials lead, true triumphs find.

Milton Keynes UK
Ingram Content Group UK Ltd.
UKHW020038271124
451585UK00012B/912

9 789916 898982